Applications of Action Learning

A Practical Guide

Copyright © George P Boulden

All Rights Reserved

No part of this book may be reproduced in any form,

by photocopying or by any electronic or mechanical means,

Including information storage or retrieval systems,

without permission in writing from both the copyright owner and the publisher of this book.

ISBN 9781791546137

First Published November 2008

ALA INTERNATIONAL PUBLISHING

Lutterworth, England - alapub@ala-international.com

Email george.boulden@ala-international.com

Web site www.ala-international.com

Ed 8 October 2019

Contents

SYNOPSIS 3
ACKNOWLEDGEMENTS 4
THE PHILOSOPHY OF ACTION LEARNING 6
    BELIEF 1 6
    BELIEF 2 9
    BELIEF 3 10
COMPONENTS OF ACTION LEARNING PROGRAMMES 12
    THE PROGRAMME 12
    THE STRUCTURE 15
    THE ROLES 17
    THE LEARNING PROCESS 19
EXAMPLE - OWN JOB PROGRAMME 28
EXAMPLE - ORGANISATIONAL CHANGE PROGRAMMES ... 35
WHAT HAVE WE LEARNED? 40
APPLICATIONS OF ACTION LEARNING IN THE 21ST CENTURY 43
FURTHER READING 45

Synopsis

Action Learning is the brain-child of Professor Reginald (Reg) Revans. Revans believed that management is a practical subject carried out by practical people in the real world of work. Not an academic subject to be taught by University Professors who had no experience of the real world of work.

Action learning uses the participant's actual job to identify and satisfy real learning needs; the specific Knowledge, Skills, Experience and Behaviour appropriate to the situation. Unlike training It provides a **'holistic'** framework through which all four aspects of our behavioural 'package' are objectively assessed by the facilitator and 'comrades in adversity' to help participants identify the things they need to change to be effective managers. These needs once identified are met through a development programme created and monitored with the help and support of the facilitator and colleagues in the set. This book;

1. Explains the philosophy of Action Learning
2. Describes the various models and their application.
3. Provides an objective analysis of the strengths and weaknesses of the various options
4. Examines how Action Learning can help in today's world to develop organisations and their people.
5. Offers reference information for those who would like to learn more.

Note. Whilst Reg's focus for Action Learning was on management development this process is equally applicable to any personal or organisational development need.

We hope you will find this book useful and are happy to help interested readers with further information or advice on specific programme design and management.

Acknowledgements

I would like to begin by acknowledging the great debt of gratitude I owe to Professor Reginald (Reg) Revans, the founder of the Action Learning movement. We met in 1974 when he was planning his first Action Learning programme in GEC. At the time of our first meeting I had recently transferred from line management into a management development role. I was very aware that mature managers did not respond well to 'teaching' and was searching for ways of creating learning opportunities. Over lunch Reg shared his ideas with me and I was sold. Thirty-five years later I am still a convinced action learner. He introduced me to Alan Lawlor who pioneered Own Job Action Learning in the West Midlands and the three of us created Action Learning Associates (ALA) Intentional in 1980 to promote the application of Action Learning. My relationship with Reg continued until his death in 2003.

I would also like to acknowledge my good friends Malcolm Farnsworth, John Cooper and Professor Steve Iman of Cal Poly Pomona CA.

Malcolm, who as Principal of the Marconi Staff Development Centre in Chelmsford, gave me the chance of a new career in management development which I have pursued for a very stimulating thirty-five years.

John, who I worked with at The Dunchurch College of Management, is a natural 'action learner' as anyone who has used or experienced the marvellous business simulations he created will testify and generous to a fault with everything he did. For me John is one of the unsung heroes of Action Learning and deserves to be recognised as such.

Steve for his encouragement and enormous contribution to the publication of the book; without Steve's guiding hand it would probably never have seen the light of day'

Finally I would like to thank the many hundreds of participants and clients from around the globe who I have learned with and from over the years. It has been a great privilege to know you, thank you all.

George P Boulden – October 2019

The Philosophy of Action Learning

Action Learning is based on Reg's three core beliefs.

Belief 1

That leaning not teaching is the key to developing people, in his case, managers. Management, he believed, is a practical subject carried out by practical people in the real world of work, not an academic subject to be taught by University Professors most of whom had never been inside a real work place.

Action Learning or Action Reflection Learning as its sometime more accurately known, means exactly what it says: learning through doing, reflecting on what one has, done to identify development needs and working to satisfy them.

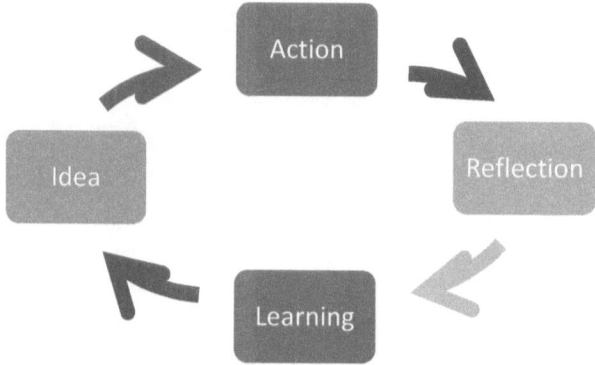

This process is at the heart of all skills training. The learner does something, the trainer reviews what is being or has been done and gives corrective guidance as appropriate until the learner demonstrates that they can do the job alone. The same process is used in coaching. The coach observes the learner and gives advice on how they can improve their performance.

There is nothing unique about 'learning through action'; skills have always been taught this way. What is unique about Action Learning was Revans application of this 'training' methodology to the process of developing managers and the role of the facilitator. In traditional training the 'trainer or coach' is a specialist in what they are training the learner to do and the aim is for the learner to emulate the trainer or coach; it's a 'push' system. The role of the facilitator in an Action Learning programme is to 'pull' the learning needs identified during the project, from the learner. Our 'real' learning needs identified through our experience, fall into four main categories;

1. Knowledge – I don't know enough about what I am trying to do. For example I have been asked to cost a proposal but don't know how to do it.
2. Skills – I have to make a presentation to a client and am not sure I have the skills to make it a 'winner'.
3. Experience – I want to create my own business but have no experience, I need some in order to get the funding I require.
4. Behaviour- I am naturally self-confident and like to get things done but recognise that my new team need more involvement.

Action learning recognises that to be successful in any given situation we need to be seen by others as having the K-S-E-B appropriate to the needs of that situation. For example if I need medical treatment for some condition I am looking for someone who clearly knows what they are doing and has demonstrated the skills to do it. In other words he/she has previous experience of the condition and makes me feel confident that all will be well.

Action Learning provides a holistic framework through which all four aspects of our behavioural 'package' are objectively assessed by the facilitator and our 'comrades in adversity' to help us identify our development needs. These are the 'barriers' to success' and once identified they can be met through a development programme created with the help and support of the facilitator and our colleagues in the set. They help us to;

> Recognise our development needs
>
> Decide to do something about them
>
> Empower us to change through 'permission'
>
> Help us create and deliver a realistic plan to achieve our development goals

Action Learning uses questioning to encourage participants to identify and commit to the action necessary to satisfy their development needs. They are then supported through the learning process by the power of the set, to achieve their learning goals; fear of looking a fool is a great motivator.

Before Revans managers were educated, post Revans we have a practical means of providing managers with training relevant to their individual needs. Revans took management education out of the classroom and put it into the work place. He changed teachers (Professors in his terms) into facilitators, students into learners rather than 'listeners' and used the jobs that participants do every day as the primary learning vehicle. He removed the syllabus and replaced it with the real world of work. He got rid of the examination and replaced it with continuous self, peer and supervisor assessment.

Belief 2

That to 'keep up' in a fast changing world we must continually question our past learning. The things that we both individually and corporately believe are based on our past experience and we must be prepared to change these beliefs if we are to successfully embrace the future. As John F Kennedy said in his famous address in the Assembly Hall at the Paulskirche in Frankfurt in 1963;

'Change is the law of life. And those who look only to the past or the present are certain to miss the   future'

Learning (L), Revans said, is determined by: -

The ability / willingness of individuals and their organisations to question (Q) their programmed knowledge (P), using the stimulus of real life problems, with the support of like minded people, the challenge provided by a facilitator and the will to reflect and learn from the action

$$L = P+Q$$

Programmed knowledge (P) is an amalgam of the knowledge, skills, experience and behaviour of individuals and organisations. It is based on 'past' experience and determines what they currently seek and seek to avoid. Looked at from one side, our 'programmed knowledge' is our strength enabling us to get things done; in conditions of rapid change however, our historically acquired knowledge, skills and behaviours are based on 'old' beliefs which are often not appropriate for survival in today's world. Anyone seeking to remain successful in our fast changing world must reflect the changing needs of those they serve. Yesterday's offering will not satisfy tomorrow's customer. Change is constant, what succeeds today, fails tomorrow.

Note This has become very clear in recent years the traditional companies who dominated the retail sector for so long are finally having to accept that low cost rivals and 'on line shopping' is here to stay.

Belief 3

That practising managers; 'comrades in adversity' as he called them, learn best with and from each other.

Action Learning creates a safe environment in which participants can test and update their P by constructively questioning themselves and others, thus allowing them their organisations to adapt to the needs of our constantly changing world. It brings people together in a supportive environment with a project; something they have agreed to do. It can be, to solve a problem or to satisfy a development need like acquiring new behavioural skills or knowledge. The project becomes the learning vehicle. With the help of the facilitator participants are asked to review how their project is going and the 'comrades in adversity' are encouraged to ask questions. These questions lead to ideas which, when tested, highlights strengths and weaknesses. Reflection on these experiences leads to new learning. The child learns that the stove is hot, not by touching it (Test), but through the pain that comes from the burn afterwards (Reflection). Learning is demonstrated if he/she does not touch the hot stove again.

The whole process is 'focused' by the 'facilitator'. He or she is there to encourage questioning, focus on action and review the learning.

Action leaning empowers people to develop themselves through: -

1. Working on a 'real life' open ended problem or development need
2. Using the experience to question what is happening and identify things they need to change
3. Agreeing actions and trying them out in practice (doing things differently)
4. Reviewing the experience and taking further actions as necessary to achieve the development goals
5. Using the experience to help others who are also learning by doing

This simple idea became what we now call 'Action Learning'. Like most new ideas it went through a process of evolution. It began in 1947 with Reg's first simple programmes with The National Coal Board in the UK. Having started however he needed the next 30 years to gain acceptance of his ideas. Many people experimented with Action Learning and added to the methodology but it was not until 1965 that he achieved a 'platform' from which to demonstrate the value of his ideas working with the Fondation Industrie-Universite in Belgium. This work led to the opportunity in 1974 for

Reg to lead a team to run the first Action Learning programme for a major UK company. GEC-Marconi as it was then was the largest electronics company in the UK with 110,000 employees around the world. The group was run by Sir Arnold Weinstock a very practical manager himself. He saw Reg explaining his ideas about Action Learning on TV. Liked what he heard, invited Reg to come and talk with him and decided that Action Learning was for him and GEC Marconi. For a detailed review of the GEC-Marconi experience I recommend that you read

More than Management Development - Edited by David Casey and David Pearce - Gower Press 1977 - ISBN0 566 02005 X

Components of Action Learning Programmes

Traditional management development programmes 'push' learning. They have a syllabus with teaching materials, which someone has decided managers need to know in order to manage effectively. Action learning on the other hand 'pulls' learning through action in the real world of work. The learning vehicle in Action Learning programmes is the project through which participants experience all that they not only need to know but also what they to be able to do in order to be an effective manager.

There are four main components to an Action Learning programme

- The programme
- The structure
- The roles
- The learning environment

The Programme

Various types of Action Learning programme have been developed over the years. These fall into two main groups, those focusing on personal development and those which focus on empowering organisational change.

Personal Development Programmes

There are four main ways in which Action Learning has been applied to Personal Development these are;

1. Own Job – The participants own job is used as the development vehicle.
2. Familiar job in different environment - Participants use their current expertise to solve a problem in an unfamiliar organization.
3. Unfamiliar job in familiar environment - Participants take on another job function, i.e. a finance manager takes

over an HR function for six months. Note. This is common in Japanese organisations.
4. Unfamiliar job in unfamiliar environment Participants work on an unfamiliar task in an unfamiliar environment.

These four models are very different and designed to satisfy different needs. The 'own job' model is by far and away the simplest and most cost effective way of applying action learning. It requires a minimum of resources, delivers job related performance improvements and does not suffer from re-entry problems or create unrealistic expectations in participants.

The other three models are all more expensive to run, resource hungry, can suffer from re-entry problems and create often unrealistic expectation in their participants. That being said, such programmes are an excellent vehicle for individual development, creating real improvements in productivity of the organisations involved and for allowing sponsors to gain a realistic assessment of a nominees potential. They are also a marvellous experience; something not to be missed if you are ever offered the opportunity!

For more information on Own Job Programmes see our book Own Job Action Learning at https://www.amazon.co.uk/dp/B018C7U2Y6. Or contact us directly

Organisational Change programmes

When I first met Reg in 1974 I had been teaching management in GEC-Marconi for over two years and had come to the conclusion that what we were doing was, in terms of its impact on the productivity of the sponsoring organisations, largely a waste of time. Yes, the participants enjoyed the training and found that the participative approach we offered to managing people was very effective but back in the workplace senior managers had no interest in productivity through involvement, the focus was on working harder not smarter. In hindsight the reason is obvious; management was not seeking productivity improvement through embracing a more participative management style. They sent their people for training because they were told to and most saw it as a short holiday rather than anything to do with the 'real world of work'.

This experience led me to realise that the behaviour of individuals is determined by the interaction between individual values and environmental values. With personal development programmes we have the whole person and they have the authority to change their values and thus their behaviour, if they feel it would be beneficial. The problem with organisational change however is that the organisation's values belong to everyone; therefore if we want to change the way the organisation functions we need to involve everyone, either directly or indirectly in the process.

I saw, in my experience with the Dunchurch Action Learning programmes, a way of using Action Learning to deliver organisational change. This I believed could be achieved by involving senior management in the programme. In practice this meant turning the senior management into an 'informal' Action Learning set facilitated by the lead consultant. Their joint project is to set targets for optimising the performance of the organisation. Thus In-Plant programmes;

1. Start at the top. Senior management are involved in agreeing the need to improve productivity, what needs to be done to improve productivity and how the successful achievement of these goals will be measured. From this a number of projects are developed with senior managers as clients.
2. Use teams made up of a representative cross section of the employees working on specific projects for their management clients. Note In these programmes the set meetings have a 'dual focus'. On the one hand they focus on working as a team to solve an organisational problem but at the same time participants are encouraged to adopt appropriate personal development goals.
3. Involve the problem solving teams not only with making the recommendations for optimising productivity but also the implementing of those recommendations which are accepted by their client and the management team. The set does not stop work until a 'fix' has actually been put in place and can be seen to be working

4. Create the conditions for the open two way communication between senior managers and the AL teams necessary to empower cultural change..

In-Plant Action Learning programmes, as we call them, are a simple way of involving *a*ll those who are or will be affected by organisational change. It allows them to find and implement 'best fit' solutions to the organisations problems thus ensuring that the chosen solution succeeds. Such programmes also provide cost effective development opportunities for large numbers of people and the inherent empowerment is great for boosting morale.

For more information see our book on In-Plant Action Learning at: https://www.amazon.co.uk/dp/B012RLDMP4 or contact us for more information

Note. The 'normal' cultural style in traditional organisations is Parent/Child. Autocracy rules; we do it to then rather than through them and are then disapointed when the children reject the parent's solution. Involvement leads to ownership, ownership creates commitment.

The structure

Typically Action Learning programmes run for about six months in five main stages:-

1. Introductory workshop. This is used to launch the programme and can vary in length from half a day to three weeks. The aim is to get things started and the more effective this process; the quicker the sets start to function effectively. Note. For personal development programmes this is usually a workshop for those who will be involved in the programme. In-Plant programmes however begin with workshop for senior management which focuses on agreeing the desired outcomes from the programme, the projects and clients.
2. Investigation and Recommendation stage. This usually runs for three months and provides the opportunity for participants to analyse the issues, to benchmark them against best practice and to produce recommendations. Note. With Own Job

programmes where the project has already been identified, like for example a need to develop leadership skills. Programmes normally last three months and begin with Implementation.
3. Presentation and Feedback. This is usually a plenary session with participants presenting their findings to their clients and clients giving an initial response. A detailed implementation programme is normally agreed later, after clients have discussed it with their colleagues.
4. Implementation. This stage also usually lasts about three months and involves participants in implementing the recommendations agreed with the client. Note. In the first part of the programme participants have a free hand to develop their recommendations. The Implementation phase however is a project in which participants work to implement recommendations which have been accepted on behalf of the client. This is a different experience because it requires action and is an essential part of the personal development process.
5. Final Review – one day. This is an opportunity to review what has / has not been learnt / achieved and to agree the way ahead.

Note - Some programmes only use the investigation phase because there is no practical outcome from the project to implement. For example, if someone is undertaking a research project they can benefit from the learning opportunities offered in the research phase but there will be nothing to implement as the outcome is the report. It is also possible, where the development need is known to use an Action Learning programme to underpin and capture the learning in the implementation phase.

Organisational change programmes are different in that threr is a specific intention to develop the organisation. Thus the measure of success of the programme is focused on how well it has achieved the desired outcomes.

See our Book on In-Plant Action Learning
https://www.amazon.co.uk/dp/B012RLDMP4 or contact us for more information

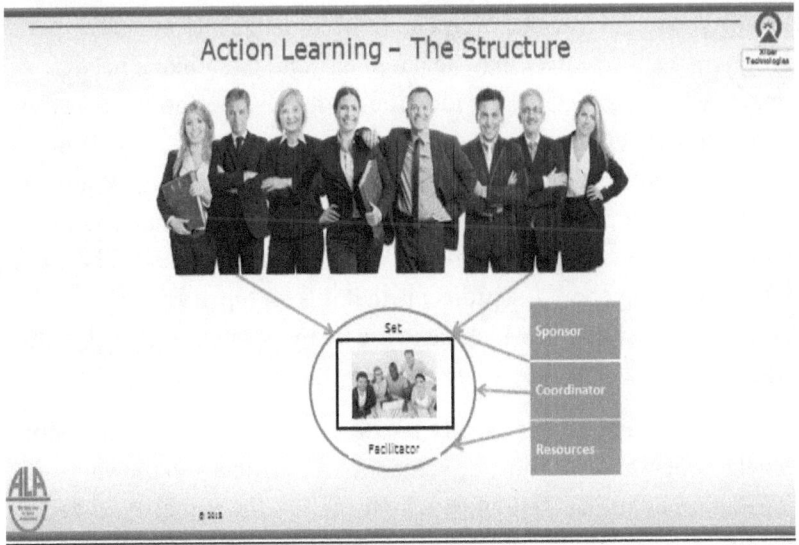

The Roles

With traditional educational programmes there are two primary roles, the teachers and the learners. In action learning programmes there are seven key roles;

Clients – are the people who own the problem / opportunity that the participants will work on. In Revan's terms this must be someone who knows, who cares, and above all, who can implement the solution recommended by the participant(s) if they wish to do so. These are senior people who believe that involving people leads to ownership which delivers commitment. These are the champions of the programme; without committed clients, there is no programme.

Participants – are the people who will participate in the programme. With Own Job programmes they are normally selected by their line manager and often he or she is also the client. For other types of personal development programme they may be selected, for example, from a talent audit, through the Performance Appraisal process and so on. In Organisational change programmes they will usually be invited as a representative of a specific work area and will represent the work groups in that area. In companies with Trades Union members will be represented as appropriate.

Projects - are the learning 'vehicle. In personal development programmes the project may be based on something like a need to improve inter personal skills identified through a performance review or a specific technical issue like improving line productivity. With In-Plant programme team projects can range from something as simple as increasing productivity by say 10% without increasing costs to launching a new product or re-structuring the organization. The most important thing about the project is that it is an 'open ended' problem, something to which there are many possible actions but no 'right answer'.

Sponsor – the sponsor is usually a senior manager who is responsible for the program. This must be someone who believes in the value of the Action Learning style of development, has the authority to deliver the programme and the money to pay for it. Note. With In-Plant programmes it will always be the CEO.

Co-ordinator – is the person responsible for the day to day administration of the programme. With an in-house programme it will normally be someone from HR in the case of open programmes it will usually be the person who sets up the programme. Note. With Organisational change programmes this is a significant role as there could be a hundred people working in ten teams all needing admin help and regular progress monitoring.

Facilitator - in Action Learning programmes is responsible for helping participants to identify and satisfy their learning needs. See the learning process for more detail.

Resources – These are the resources needed to satisfy the development needs identified during the project. Some will be available within the set. For example if one member is having problems understanding a costing & budgeting situation and there is another member in the set who is an accountant he/she may volunteer to help with the problem or if all set members feel that a better understanding of the numbers would be beneficial they may ask the facilitator to organise a workshop and extend the time of the next meeting to accommodate it. It is also possible that the facilitator has some relevant knowledge, skills or experience they are prepared to share. In some cases it will be necessary for participants to seek outside help through short courses or a short secondment to gain experience et al. The organisation may create a learning Resource Centre to support the sets or negotiate a contract with a local College of Management to provide resources on an 'as and when' basis.

The Learning Process

Traditionally managers were taught about management; but they were not taught how to manage. Management development meant attending a training programme with a syllabus based on what the delivering organisation believed managers needed to know, not what they needed to be able to do.

Reg believed that managers are practical people who need to solve practical problems in the real world of work. He believed that whilst the study of management may be interesting, and for me it certainly was; however it had little relevance to the daily grind of management. So rather than assume what managers needed to know, Reg believed that that we should ask them to identify their needs and then help them to satisfy them. But how could this be achieved in a practical way?

The answer was simple; he decided to give them a project based on something they were trying to achieve in their own jobs. To reinforce the value of the project he decided that they should share their project with their supervisor who would be asked to authorise the project, hold regular progress reviews and provide support both financial and moral support to achieve a successful outcome.

But this was not enough. The 'coup de grace' of Action Learning is the set; what Reg called his 'comrades in adversity'. These are groups of between five and seven people who shared their projects and meet regularly to share their experiences and learn with and from each other.

This learning model has developed over the years and 'learning' is now the responsibility of the facilitator.

This is usually an external person whose main area of expertise lies in helping others to help themselves.

The facilitator must understand;

1. The four components of competence
2. The nature and process of change
3. How to help others commit to helping themselves

The four 'components' of competence

The role of the facilitator is firstly to help participants to identify from the experience gained on their project to identify their development needs. To do this we recommend using the four 'components' of competence. These are;

1. Knowledge, what we need to know
2. Skills, what we need to be able to do
3. Experience we need to be able to demonstrate to others that we are capable
4. Behaviour; the ability to communicate appropriately in different situations

Knowledge – What do we know now that is relevant to our future? What do we know/believe that is not relevant to our future? What do we not know/ believe now that is necessary for our future?

Skills – What can we do now that is relevant to our future? What can we do now that is not relevant to our future? What can we not do now that is necessary for our future?

Experience – What experience do we have now that is relevant to our future? What experience do we have that is not relevant to our future? What experience do we not have now that is necessary for our future?

Behaviour – What behaviours do we have now that are relevant to our future? What behaviours do we have now that that is not appropriate to our future? What behaviours do we need to acquire to be successful in the future?

The nature and process of change

Having done this the second step is to help them commitment to doing something about the needs which have been identified using the for step model;

Our current behavior, the way we handle the different situations we meet in our daily lives, is determined by our values seen through the eyes of our environment We use the learned behaviors from our past to respond to what is happening now, and the results that we achieve from our actions are used to reinforce our role models. This is a closed loop; if I get something right, I have done well, and if it goes wrong, it's usually someone else's fault. Thus, under normal circumstances, our attitudes and behavior are self-sustaining; to change we have to break the loop, which means questioning the appropriateness of some current action or belief.

The four-step process of change:

1. **Recognition**—of the need for change; that something we are doing or believe in is inappropriate to our desired outcomes.
2. **Decision**—being prepared to commit to do something about the things we need to change.
3. **Permission**—obtaining the permission to change through appropriate role models and coaching support.
4. **Action**—putting in place and working through the steps necessary to achieve the desired result.

Recognition

To be successful in life, we must be prepared to commit ourselves to a path of ongoing learning. This means assessing both our successes and failures to understand those things we do well and need to do more of and those things that done differently would produce more desirable outcomes. Such feedback can be "internal," something that we recognize about ourselves, or it can be "external," based on the observations of others. For example, I may recognize the need to reduce my weight when I stand on the bathroom scales or maybe when a friend says, "Put on a bit of weight recently George?" Either input can influence me to think about shedding a few pounds before venturing onto the beach. Feedback that is strong enough to make us question our current behavior creates the possibility of change.

If we accept that some aspect of our current behaviors or beliefs are inappropriate, we have two options; we can accept the feedback, in which case we move on to the first step of the change ladder, which is **recognition,** or we can reject the input by **rationalizing** it.

Some years ago I was flying with what was then recognized as one of the world's leading airlines in terms of passenger care. The meal was served with style, and the wines were good; unfortunately, the meat was tough and almost cold, but not bad enough to complain. Later the head steward came through the cabin, asking passengers if they had enjoyed their meal; when it was my turn, I explained that I had been a little disappointed. His immediate reaction was that he was sorry that I didn't like my meal but that all the other passengers he had spoken to were satisfied! If you don't want feedback, you should not ask for it.

Note. Clearly not all feedback is objective or relevant, and the ability to rationalize it is, I believe, a key factor in maintaining our self-worth. However, if it is overdone, it becomes a barrier to learning.

I would like to stress again at this point that in my view, human behavior should not be thought of in terms of right and wrong but as appropriate or inappropriate to the situation. The way we react may well have been appropriate in earlier times or different situations but may be inappropriate now because circumstances have changed.

Decision

The second step is making the **decision** to do something about the thing(s) we have identified as no longer appropriate. Making such decisions is easy, but the problem is implementation. It is easy for me to decide to start my new diet on Sunday, but unfortunately when Sunday comes, I realize that it's a "ham and eggs" day, and I love my ham and eggs, so maybe next Sunday! I made the decision to go on a diet but am not prepared to make the necessary sacrifice to do it. There can be no gain without pain as the saying goes, so if you really want a new you, there are going to be sacrifices. To be successful we must not only decide but be prepared to commit to what we decide. So it's important to be realistic; it's much better to start small and grow big than to start big and fail. Note. We can strengthen our resolve by sharing our decision with others; this increases the pressure on us to act as we don't want to be seen as a failure!

Permission

If I am committed to the **decision** to reduce my weight, stop smoking, improve my golf, get a new job, open my own business, and so on, I need **permission**. Permission is the third step in the process of change and is necessary for two reasons:

Our current behaviors and beliefs have been reinforced by apparently successful application throughout our lives. If we are now saying that some of our behaviors are "inappropriate" to our current situation, we need some "authority" to change them.

Secondly we reduce the risk of failure if we follow the experience of others who have successfully done what we want to do; their success permits us to do it and can be used to guide us through the process.

We obtain permission by finding role models—people who have successfully done what we want to do before. This can come from reading a book; talking to someone who has done it; seeking help from an expert, a professional to improve your golf, or a lifestyle coach to get you back in shape; or joining one of the plethora of specialist focus groups catering for most everyday changes, like stopping smoking, drinking, dieting, fitness, and so on.

Some years ago I decided to walk the Pennine Way. This is a path that runs for 412 kilometers through the Pennine Hills in the north of England, from just north of Manchester to southern Scotland. The first thing I did was to speak with someone I knew who had walked half of it; the second was to buy a guidebook written by a recognized expert on the subject, and the third was to start walking the five kilometers to work every day to get used to wearing my new boots! Role models give us permission to change; they offer a methodology, a structured approach for achieving our change, and they provide support to keep us going when things get tough.

Action

The fourth step in the change process is **action**, but it's more than just action. It's about delivery—taking the actions necessary to deliver the desired outcomes. So action is about planning, implementing, monitoring, and controlling.

The action or actions you take will clearly depend on what you have decided to change. This can be something as simple as losing weight (simple does not mean easy!). This is something you can "buy" into as it's already "packaged," and there will normally be a number of competing suppliers. So the first step will be to create some criteria, which will allow you to objectively assess the different options. This will include things like price, supplier reputation, convenience—travel, hours, and so on. The next step is to look at what is on offer, compare the offerings against your criteria, and choose a supplier. Implementation in this example means signing on. Once on board you will have weight-loss targets, which you can use to monitor progress, and the group leader will be on hand to encourage and "control" your achievement?

Helping others commit to helping themselves

In Action Learning programmes the facilitator has two roles; he/she coordinates the set meetings and facilitates the learning. Set meetings follow a 'standard' procedure. The facilitator, acting as coordinator welcomes everyone; then invites one participant at a time to, in the first meeting, share their projects and their proposed actions and in subsequent meetings what they have done against their plan since the last meeting. The review then moves on to a discussion of what has gone well and why? This is followed by the participant being encouraged to reflect on what has not gone so well and why? Note. It is particularly important to look for 'rationalisation' at this stage and probe to find the 'real' reason. The things that do not go well are the pointers to the participant's learning needs and must be fully explored to create understanding from which Areas for Improvement (AFI's) can be agreed.

Each participant usually has 20/30 minutes of personal 'air time'. Group members are encouraged to question and share relevant experiences, with the focus on the actions they took to resolve similar issues and the results achieved. Note. It is a good idea to change the order in which group members report back from meeting to meeting.

Time keeping is important. All members are entitled to their share of the 'air time' so the co-ordinator needs to encourage members to work through their agenda's in the allotted time. If something of general interest comes up it can be moved to the end of the session.

Set members are encouraged to question their colleagues; helping others to identify their learning process is a key skill which all members should be encouraged to acquire. The facilitator listens carefully to what is being said and the way it is said to ensure understanding. "I almost got it right" does not have the same meaning as "I got it right". They encourage questioning, particularly the use of open questions and carefully monitor the body language to ensure that all members are actively listening to what is going on. If some members don't appear to be involved the facilitator should not hesitate to bring them in. Similarly if a member looks unhappy with the way the discussion is going but is not saying very much the facilitator might say - "Fred, you don't look very happy..." Making sure that everyone in involved and that all views are brought out into the open ensures good quality debate which helps the learner to identify his/her development needs.

Note. Reg said on many occasions that he felt it was not necessary to use 'professional' facilitators. Sets he said, can facilitate themselves and in my experience he was right. Facilitation is a natural process; it's the way we obtain 'permission' to change our lives. Virtually all of us have both used others to facilitate our change and have facilitated others in their change; we just didn't know we were doing it! However, whilst I agree with him in principle, in practice I believe that sets need external facilitation at the start of the process. They need someone who knows what they are doing to 'get them going'; once they are familiar with the process they can and will facilitate their own learning.

Our approach, once the set understand the role, is to ask them to rotate both the Meeting Coordinator and the Facilitation role. This gives all members an additional learning opportunity which most find very rewarding. See following case study.

Note – It is very important that proposed projects are evaluated before a programme begins to ensure that they are real and embody the opportunity for the participant to do something that will have a real impact the performance of the organisation.

For a more detailed explanation on the role of the facilitator and an introduction to some of tools used for analysing group behaviour please see our book Empowering Change through Facilitation
https://www.amazon.co.uk/dp/B015RE6ASY

Example - Own Job Programme

Case – Using the Own Job Model in personal development

In 2000 Roche Pharma introduced, with London Business School, the 'Insights for Pharma' program. Insights was a one week 360- leadership development program designed to develop Pharma senior managers as leaders. Pharma (PD) supported the program and carried out a research project on its effectiveness early 2002. The study found that whilst the vast majority of participants felt that the workshop itself had been personally satisfying, many reported having difficulty applying their newly discovered leadership skills back in the workplace. PD management had already embraced the idea that enhanced leadership was the best way to optimize performance in difficult market conditions. They decided to build on the Insights for Pharma program by introducing Own Job action learning, they called it, Peer Group Learning (PGL), as a vehicle for providing local support for those Insights participants who wished to develop their leadership competencies in their working environment.

It was decided to start the programme by inviting all past participants of the Insights workshops to join a Peer Group Learning set. Of the 95 Insights alumni who were invited 75 attended introductory meetings and 49 across the three main sites decided to participate in the pilot program enabling nine sets to be created. In parallel with the launch of the program twelve people from the HR community were recruited and trained as facilitators. The training of this group involved a short introductory workshop on the PGL (Action Learning) philosophy followed by on job training. Once the sets had been created, the internal facilitators, supported by an external specialist, held one on one meetings with set members. These meetings had two main objectives:

1. To develop set member's understanding of the PGL process, how it worked and to answer any queries they may have

2. To help participants reframe the development needs identified during the Insights workshop into something achievable and relevant to the development need.

The following is a typical example:

The Project -   To develop a more participative style of Management

The Issues - I tended to dominate meetings
Worse with certain topics / areas
Needed to be more reflective
Be more of a "plant"
Wanted to practice facilitation skills
Increase active listening skills

Achievements -   Let others chair Departmental meetings & facilitate them
Ask for regular feedback from peers on the senior management team
Wait to be asked to contribute more
Used Myers Briggs to understand more about myself and my team

Facilitated a PGL set

Keep a weekly "I did this well this week" list.

Set meetings began in January 2003. Typically these started with the facilitator outlining the aims of PGL. Set members then appointed a coordinator for the meeting and agreed individual 'air time'. Participants were encouraged to share their development projects and to set out their action plans. The main points of each person's plan were recorded by the coordinator to be used as the agenda for the next meeting. The facilitator encouraged open discussion and members very quickly developed a good open relationship, with lots of sharing experience and ideas.

Meetings continued at the rate of about one a month, usually at lunch time as this reduced the time away from the job, with most people attending. On a number of occasions people who could not attend participated by telephone. One set had two members from Italy and apart from the first meeting, used video conferencing to communicate.

A review of the program with participant's facilitators and sponsoring managers was carried out on all three sites during the week beginning 19th May by which time most sets had had six meetings.

Our findings show that all participants both enjoyed the experience and reported that they had been successful in achieving their development goals with more than 50% having begun a second phase of development. They valued the discipline imposed by the PGL meetings, the facilitation, and the opportunity to share experiences and to learn with and from each other. The feedback shows that PGL is seen by the participants as being key to enabling them to achieve their learning goals. 86% reported the overall value of the PGL process as good or excellent. The main strengths pf PGL were seen as:

1. Providing a safe environment
2. Giving access to relevant support materials
3. The facilitation which encouraged participants to question themselves and others
4. An opportunity to share and learn with and from each other
5. Demonstrating   management support

The following comments made during the review meetings provide a good summary of participant's views on PGL:

1. Drives forward action plans - brings focus and relevance
2. The 'team' provides a positive obligation to change
3. Structured time - scheduled/agenda/ notes etc / actions
4. Gave access to a supportive group
5. Demonstrated that the more you put in, the more everyone gets out
6. Provides resources - internal, share web, training facilities, external ALA adviser + materials
7. Became a valuable forum for - sharing ideas confidentially - questioning assumptions
8. A focus for networking / sharing - time saving as not reinventing the wheel
9. Created time to talk and reflect about people issues
10. A forum for honest communication and experience of trust (not found in our normal work teams)

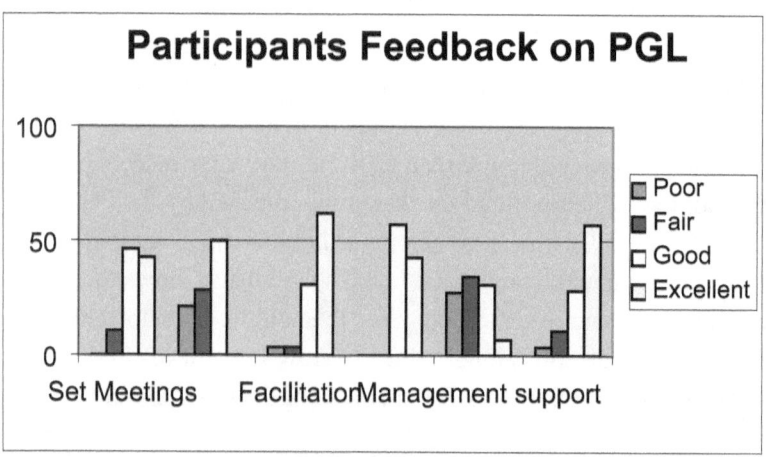

The facilitators reported that they have learnt by doing. They enjoyed the experience and felt they now have the confidence to work alone. All said the experience was either good or excellent. They valued the training they received; however a number said they would have liked a longer period of formal up-front training. 70% felt comfortable with the re-framing process; however 25% felt that this needs improvement. Set meetings are seen as very valuable but there are mixed views as to the value of the support materials. The facilitators value highly the external facilitation support they have received.

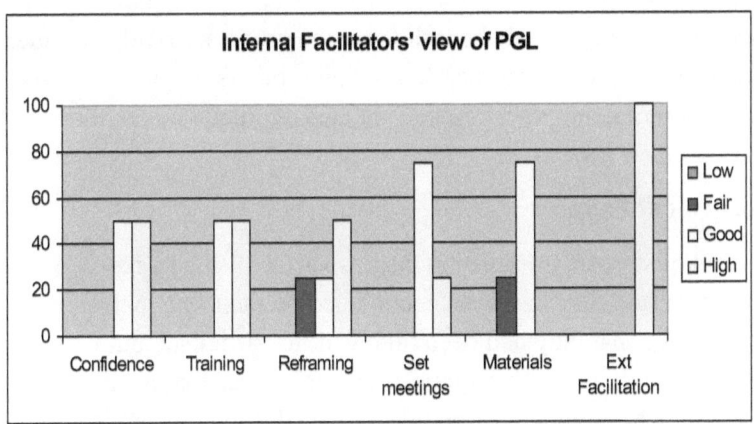

The main issues were:

Time pressure

This was seen as major issue. Participants were all very busy and many reported that they had difficulty finding (making) the time to attend meetings. There was a feeling that management should 'allocate time' for working in PGL sets. The organisers disagreed with this view. Time is always an issue for busy people but we always find the time to do the things we believe are important. Having someone 'approve' spending time developing one's self does not create the motivation necessary for success. Making the time for self-development is part of being a leader. Making the decision to participate is the first step in the self-development process; if people are committed they will make the time to meet; the people in the nine pilot sets have, which speaks for itself.

Diversity/Make-up of the sets

It was felt that the sets had worked well with a good 'chemistry' being quickly established between members. Having people from different work areas was seen as important in ensuring a good mix.

There were also some concerns about the life cycle of the sets, when should they stop and how this should be managed. About half of the original sets have already decided to continue up to Christmas and see; the others plan to meet again in September to decide.

Future projects

Concerns were expressed about the way the process should continue. Some would like to see further 360 reviews; others would like to see the adoption of a more performance related approach linked the Annual Review Process.

Management Support

The level of support from line managers varied. Whilst a few participants said they had been encouraged by their line managers most reported that they had been 'allowed' to participate but had received little, if any active support. This is an area that needs some thought; line managers must be fully engaged if the process is to lead to real long-term change. Line managers had not been part of PGL (or Insights) and whilst they were invited to the PGL introductory and review meetings, few responded. We encouraged participants to share their development plans with their line managers. Some did and received good support; others have not, for a variety of reasons. There is an issue of lack of trust here, which affects productivity directly and negatively, the situation needs to be reviewed and a formal policy on the line manger's role in developing their direct reports agreed. Note. *We feel that some of the problem here may be due to the matrix structure of PD in which people have both line and project managers. Whilst project managers accept the responsibility for technical training of staff it is unclear who is responsible for personal development.*

From the evidence we concluded that the prime aim of the pilot project, to introduce the concept and practice of Peer Group Learning into Roche PD, had been achieved at all sites. The feedback indicated that PGL is able to deliver the stated long-term aim; to contribute to the growth of a learning culture within Roche by enabling participants to develop their leadership skills. Those who participated said they felt that PGL: *"Shows   that management value us."*

They saw the PGL's and the Leadership Team support this implied, as a clear indication that management has changed its approach to the way they manage us; they are now encouraging us to change". When asked what they would say to management about PGL they said: *"Thank you!"*

As a result of the experience management felt that PGL had shown itself to be a simple, effective process for helping people to develop themselves. It was well suited to the Roche culture and style of working. It was therefore decided to formerly adopt PGL it formally as part of Leadership development and link it seamlessly with Insights.

Example - Organisational Change Programmes

Case 1 – Restructuring using the In-plant Method

A large Information Systems department of a nation-wide retail organisation found themselves in the position of having increasingly heavy demands placed on their services. In the past increases in demand were met by an increase in the number of personnel working in the department. The management of the department, however, decided that they wanted to use the existing resources more efficiently to cope with the expanding workload. The management team decided that being more efficient would mean:

Restructuring from an 'application teams' base in which dedicated teams support specific applications to a 'project teams' base with 'pools' of resources being allocated to various projects and applications on an as required basis introducing a more rigorous project control system.

There were however, a number of barriers to introducing these changes:

1. The department was structured 'traditionally' into teams each dedicated to the support of a particular application. These dedicated teams had developed considerable expertise in their various systems but their knowledge was not always well documented. Restructuring to a project focused structure raised concerns about the possible loss of expertise in key areas.
2. The teams were well established and had a strong sense of camaraderie associated with them. This, coupled with a fear of redundancy caused by the economic climate, may have generated a resistance to change.
3. The increased demand had not by then affected delivery to 'customers' and therefore the pressure to change was, at the time, purely an internal one.

The issue was how to:

1. Move to a more flexible and efficient structure
2. At the same time implement better project control
3. Do so with the willing co-operation of the work force.

Our initial aim was to create the conditions for change so we suggested a three-stage programme starting with a two-day workshop for the first two layers of management (about thirty people in all). During the workshop the team agreed their vision for the department (what it is trying to achieve and how it should go about achieving it). The topics discussed included:

1. The guiding philosophy to be used to reach the vision
2. The structures needed to achieve the vision
3. The roles that would be necessary to deliver our service
4. The systems and procedures required to manage the function
5. The work that needs to be done to assess the viability of what has been discussed

In the following phase the next two levels of management in the structure were formed into action learning sets and were then asked to carry out projects to investigate the feasibility of the vision proposed by the top team.

Each senior manager became a *'Client'* for a specific project. This meant that they were responsible for ensuring that the work was carried out in a timely manner and that any 'road blocks' or 'political obstacles' were removed from their team's path. The project sets all received one day's training and then began working part time on their projects.

The sets met fortnightly and their meetings were attended by *'Facilitators'* whose role it was to:

1. Give general guidance to the teams

2. Encourage team working
3. Ensure that individual team members received support for their personal development needs.

Facilitators and clients met once a month to review the team's overall progress. After three months the sets presented their findings to the top team.

The third stage involved the top team reviewing the results of the project work and deciding the way ahead. In this case that meant actually changing the organisation structure, putting in place a new project management system and using the sets to help manage the changes.

As a result of the approach taken there was a high degree of 'buy in' to the changes by the work force as a whole. The need to do things differently was accepted and the restructuring that was decided upon was generally perceived as both fair and appropriate. The changes were implemented successfully using the project teams providing management with a department appropriately structured and a workforce motivated to meet the challenges ahead.

Case 2 - Improving Customer Satisfaction

The senior managers of a large service organisation were concerned that a recent round of redundancies had damaged the morale of remaining employees and that attitudes to customer care had been weakened. There was evidence of employees 'talking down the company' and being reluctant to take the initiative and respond positively to business and customer needs. As a result the senior managers wanted to launch an initiative that would encourage service personnel to identify more closely with the company, create a culture of seeking to satisfy customers and empower employees to tackle some of the issues facing them.

The ALA programme to meet these aims began with all members of the service function attending a half-day workshop. The event started with the Head of Service making a keynote speech on the issues facing the function with particular reference to customer relationships. The delegates then listed the key issues that were affecting customer relationships, as they saw them. Then designed a questionnaire to measure the impact of these issues and agreed a plan for carrying out a customer survey.

The participants were formed into action learning sets and each set was allocated part of the survey. Over the next four weeks each set conducted its part the survey in the field. One member from each set then attended a one-day workshop were the survey results were collated and analysed. The sets then met again for half a day during which time the results of the survey were discussed and the problems prioritised. Each set then agreed to take responsibility for solving one of the problems and was given a one-day course in problem solving before starting work. Senior managers became the *clients* for the sets and the middle manager became the *set facilitators*.

The sets worked on their problem for three months and then formally presented their findings to their clients. Most of the suggested actions were accepted immediately though top management asked for additional work to be done on a number of points. Over the next three months the sets began to implement those recommendations which had been accepted. By the time of the final review a sea change of attitudes had taken place, thanks in large part to a strong *sponsor* in the shape of the Service Director.

At the start of the initiative many employees were hostile. They felt that management did not listen to them and that any attempt to involve them in problem solving would be a sham; nothing would change. In addition, many middle managers felt that the time spent on group problem solving was a complete waste of effort and that employees should be 'fixing units' and not be concerned with procedures and work practices. They also doubted their employees' willingness and ability to do anything about the problems they had chosen to work on.

As the programme progressed and the momentum behind it was not watered down, employees began to have more and more trust in the management of the company. As the sets continued with their work the middle managers began to appreciate the contribution to resolving problems that the employees were capable of making. By the end of the programme customer satisfaction levels had improved markedly as key problems were fixed and employees' confidence and trust in one another grew. Due to the cross-functional nature of the teams many internal 'walls' were broken down and a number of 'spin off' improvements were made. For example, as a result of the survey work, one department reorganised on the basis of 'key customer accounts' rather than geographical location.

Please see our book 'Empowering Organisational Change for a more detailed explanation.

Applications of Action Learning

What Have We Learned?

On the positive side, after over thirty years working with Action Learning it is clear that:

1. Action learning is 'holistic'. It develops the whole person; Knowledge, Skills, Experience and Behaviour
2. It can cost but it can be cost neutral or 'value adding' depending on the projects
3. It empowers people to be; removes the barriers created in childhood and allows participants to live their dreams
4. Pulling learning through; identifying real learning needs in practice is far better than pushing it through a syllabus. People seeking to satisfy goals they set for themselves are more highly motivated to learn than those who have learning goals set for them.
5. People; more crucially their organisations and their leaders need to learn the new paradigms faster than the rate of change. Organisations that do not stay ahead of the wave of change are swamped by it. Action Learning provides the environment for continual challenge and ongoing, incremental change.
6. Empowered employees at all levels are our only hope for the future. Action Learning involves people; involvement leads to ownership which delivers commitment and through this enhanced productivity.
7. Practical people in the real world of work 'Comrades in Adversity' as Reg called them really do learn best with and from each other.

These are the 'plus' points. There are, however, a number of issues with Action Learning which anyone contemplating using it needs to be aware of:

1. The lack of structure, no syllabus, no examinations, can make it difficult to 'sell'. A 'normal' training programme delivered

in a normal way is a much 'safer' proposition for organisations that want to avoid risk.
2. Some participants just don't like action reflection learning. They don't like having to agree targets in the set against which they will later be assessed. Others, the more insecure among us don't like the group aspect as they feel exposed when asked to share and to 'get involved'.
3. Some sponsoring managers don't like the empowerment aspect. They seem to find the empowerment of employees threatening, undermining their authority to manage.
4. The process can be seen as time consuming. Having people off the job for four hours a month can be seen as a problem by some more controlling managers. Note - I take the view that managers and supervisors should be responsible for how they spend their time. They are responsible for what others do; surely they should be responsible for themselves!
5. Participants who identify organisational issues that they are unable to change, like inter-departmental rivalries, empire building, management's unwillingness to adopt a more open style etc., can decide to leave.
6. People can become frustrated if management fail to support the programme. This is a particular problem with In-Plant programmes when senior managers find the teams' recommendations threatening to their empires and fail to support to proposed changes.
7. It's easy to 'deny' the value of the experience; to see it as only a programme, with a start, middle and end. When it does end we can go back to doing what we did before and those who don't like it can leave!

All of these issues I believe reflect cultural values. Western culture values individualism, Eastern cultures on the other hand tend to value 'corporate' success. My fifteen years working in Japan has shown me that for the Japanese and I understand that this is an Asian trait; corporate success is synonymous with personal success. In practice these cultural differences mean that whilst empowerment models like 5's, Waste Weeding, Quality Circles, Total Productivity Maintenance

(TPM) and Action Learning work well in Eastern cultures they are not so easily accepted in the West.

In my experience, empowerment works well at the functional level in Western companies; most workers like being involved in the decision making process; Western managements however do not like being 'advised' by their 'subordinates'. Action Learning offers a powerful set of tools for helping management to optimise the performance of both individuals and their organisations, the problem lies in persuading management to use them!.

Applications of Action Learning in the 21st Century

Action Learning is the most effective development tool available to those organisations seeking to optimise the potential of their resources through the empowerment of their people.

The four individual development models allow a range of personal development goals to be achieved, ranging from improving expertise in the participants current post to gaining an understanding of different functions and business units. From a purely practical point of view we would suggest that the two most practical options are the Own Job and Exchange programmes.

Own Job programmes offer the most cost effective and least risk option. People stay in their own jobs; there are no re-entry problems and what the participants can use what they learn. The only requirement is to ensure that nominating mangers understand the process and their role in supporting their participants through the learning experience.

Exchange programmes are mainly appropriate to the development of senior specialist manager who the organisation would like to 'broaden' with a view to them taking up more senior positions in the future. Such programmes will normally be full time, focus on 'strategy' and be based at a Management Centre where there is a wide range of expertise available to participants. Whilst such programmes are expensive they do provide very powerful development opportunities for participants and an opportunity for sponsors to objectively assess the potential of those attending for more senior positions.

In-plant Action Learning programmes are ideally suited for delivering cultural change whilst at the same time providing a cost effective development opportunity for large numbers of people. To be successful these programmes need the commitment of senior management, which, in practice means that they must be clear what they want as an outcome. Over the years we worked on a number of Quality Circles programmes and it was clear that whilst managements wanted quality, they didn't want Quality Circles meeting and highlighting the management deficiencies which impact quality! Empowering employees is not something that can be switched on and off without cost. If management would like employees to help introduce major changes into an organisation successful outcomes must be recognised and ongoing procedures for appropriate empowerment must be built into the culture. Quality Circles, 5's, TPM etc. are not projects they are life style changes

If you would like to design a programme, or like to know more about Action Learning please contact us, we will be happy to help.

Further Reading

If you have found reading this book interesting you may also find the following useful.

1. For an insight into human behaviour I recommend Dr. Thomas A. Harris is the author of *I'm OK – You're OK*, the 1969 bestseller based upon the ideas of Transactional Analysis by Dr Eric Berne. ISBN 0-06-072427. If you find this interesting you may also like to read 'The Games People Play, by Dr Eric Berne ISBN 0-345-41003-3

2. In the same géndre but more focused on 'rapport' skills is NPL, How to Build a Successful Life by Richard Brandler, Alessio Roberti & Owen Fitzpatrick, published by Harper Collins, ISBN 978-0-00-749741-6

3. For a deeper understanding of values I suggest 'What Matters Most' by Hyrum W Smith, published by Franklin Covey Co. ISBN 0-684-87256-0

4. For an entertaining insight into the real world of influencing I recommend the book 'When I Stop Talking You'll Know I'm Dead by Jerry Weintraub, Rich Cohen and George Clooney, Published by Hachette Books ISBN 978-0-446-54815-1

5. To learn more about 'action learning' I recommend Reg's original book on the subject 'The ABC of Action Learning' Published by Gower Publications, ISBN 978-1-4094-2703-2. Mike Pedlar's Action Learning in Practice, Third Edition, Ed Mike Pedler, Gower Press, ISBN 0 566 07795 7 and More than Management Development, Edited by David Casey & David Pearce, Gower Press, 1977. ISBN 0-566-022005-X This book reviews the early GEC programmes referred to in this text.

6. If you would like to learn more about Facilitation then 'Facilitating Action Learning: A Practitioner's Guide'

by <u>Mike Pedler</u> and <u>Christine Abbott</u> is a useful read. Also David Casey's excellent paper on The Emerging Role of the Set Advisers, copies available from ALA International

Books George has written on Action Learning and related topics

The following books are published by ALA International. they are available on our web site www.ala-international.com and from **Google Books** and **Amazon** in Epub or paperback formats.

Books about Action learning

Applications of Action Learning – describes the philosophy of action learning and its applications. ISBN 978-0-9560822-4-4

Own Job Action Learning – describes how Action learning can be used in individual development programmes. ISBN 978-0-9560822-0-6

In-Plant Action Learning – explains how the philosophy of Action learning can be used to deliver organisational change. ISBN 978-0-9560822-3-7

In-Plant Action Learning Teams, Participants Guide – This Guide is designed to help In-Plant teams to self-manage and facilitate their own learning; available from ALA International.

Empowering Change through Facilitation – describes how the process of facilitation is used to develop participants in Action Learning sets. ISBN 978-0 -9560822-9-9

Books about Personal Development

Managers as Leaders - This book show how management and leadership combine to ensure the effective delivery of the task. ISBN 978-0-9560822-2-0

Managing Difficult Relationships – examines the reasons for difficult relationships and provides a 'framework' for negotiating win / win solutions. ISBN 978-0-9560822-5-1

Change; Become a Winner - I believe that life is not a rehearsal, it's a journey and you can change it. If you would like to do something different with your life this book is for you. ISBN 13 978-1503185401, ISBN 10:1503185400

Books about Productivity

Values & Style; the Key to Productivity –The common denominator in performance improvement in organizations, is managing style. The things that stop people doing the best job they can stem from 'them and us' attitudes. These are based on cultural values and determine the way human beings perceive their roles and relationships within hierarchies. This book explores the nature of values and style and how they impact the operating effectiveness of organizations and societies.

Re-Engineering the Workplace – This book describes the Japanese approach to productivity with practical examples on how it can be applied in practice.

Useful web sites for Action Learning

Action Learning is a worldwide network. The following are some useful contacts in the Action Learning world:-

The International Foundation for Action Learning (IFAL), formally The Action Learning Trust www.ifal.org.uk

International Community of Action Learners (ICAL) This is a loose federation of Action Learning practitioners. Their web site can be found on www.tlainc.com

IMC acts as a clearing house for academic institutions offering Action Learning programmes. Contact www.imc.org.uk/imcal-inter For articles www.free-press.com/journals/gaja

The Revans Library at Salford University www.salford.ac.uk

World Institute for Action Learning, www.wial.com

Global Executive Learning – Formed in 1996 this international organisation focus on the use of Action Learning to deliver business solutions. http://www.global-executive-learning.com/index.php/en/2013-08-29-11-59-43/our-foundation

Wikipedia – https://en.wikipedia.org/wiki/Action_learning

Nursing Times http://www.nursingtimes.net/nursing-practice/specialisms/educators/how-to-use-action-learning-sets-to-support-nurses/5044296.article

Please use the following link to find our books on Amazon.

http://www.amazon.com/s?ie=UTF8&page=1&rh=n%3A283155%2Cp_27%3AGeorge%20Boulden

I will be very grateful if you take a few minutes to write a review on this book while you are there. Thank you.

George Boulden

www.ingramcontent.com/pod-product-compliance
Lightning Source LLC
Chambersburg PA
CBHW030537220526
45463CB00007B/2868